MERMAIDS

by Marya Patrice Sherron

Black Girl

MAGIC

Doodle Journal

You
Are Beautiful.

What's in Your Thought Bubble Today?

DATE:

Never Stop Dreaming.

What's in Your Thought Bubble Today?

DATE:

Magic is
Everywhere.

What's in Your Thought Bubble Today?

DATE:

_____

_____

_____

_____

_____

_____

_____

_____

_____

_____

_____

_____

_____

_____

_____

_____

_____

_____

_____

Believe in
Yourself.

What's in Your Thought Bubble Today?

DATE:

_____

_____

_____

_____

_____

_____

_____

_____

_____

_____

_____

_____

_____

_____

_____

_____

_____

_____

Dance Every Day.

What's in Your Thought Bubble Today?

DATE:

Let Your Inner
Mermaid Out.

What's in Your Thought Bubble Today?

DATE:

Gratitude Changes
'Things.

What's in Your Thought Bubble Today?

DATE:

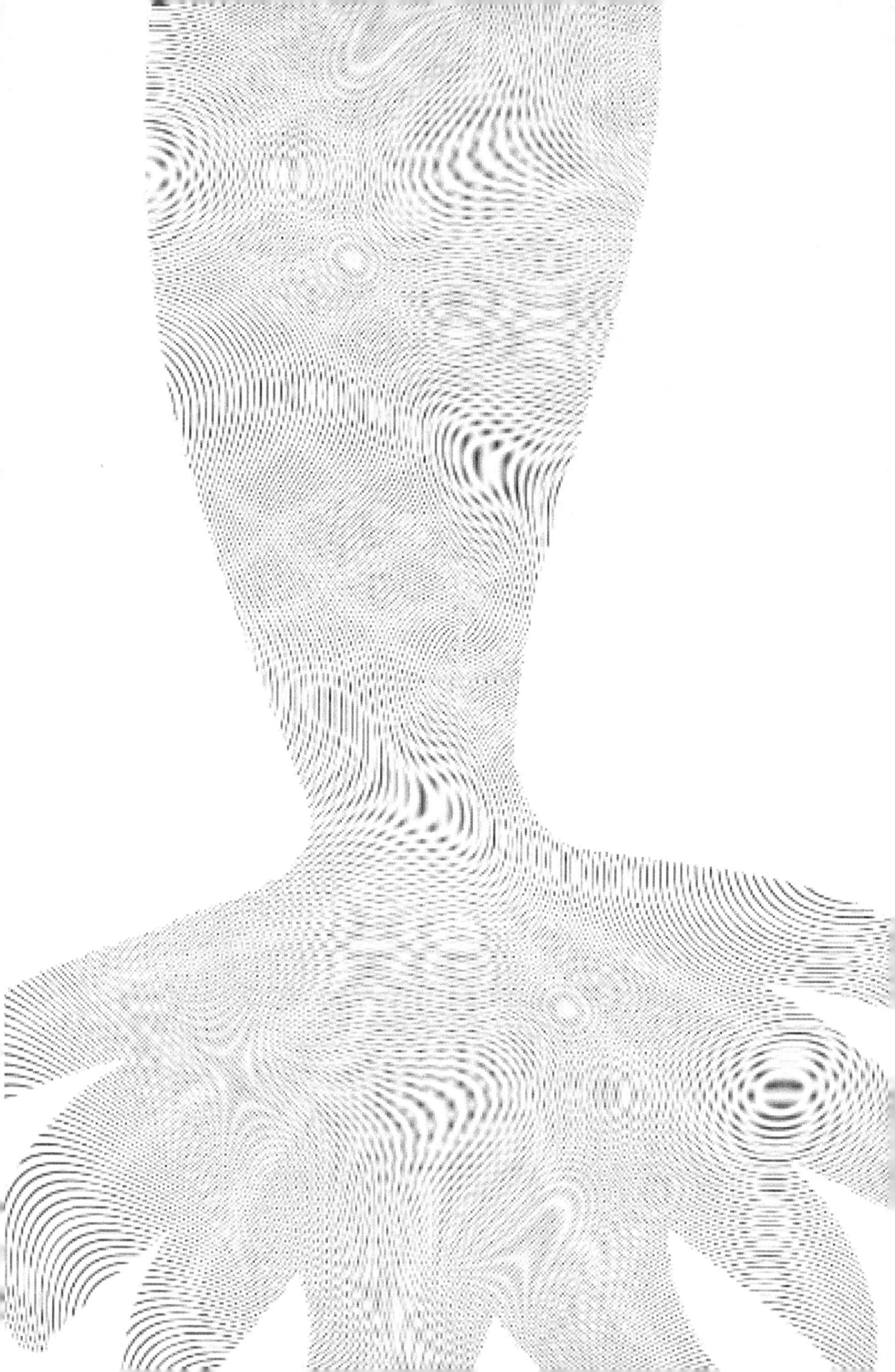

Seek Adventure &
Always Explore.

What's in Your Thought Bubble Today?

DATE:

_____

_____

_____

_____

_____

_____

_____

_____

_____

_____

_____

_____

_____

_____

_____

_____

_____

Even Seashells
Have a Story.
What's Yours?

What's in Your Thought Bubble Today?

DATE:

_____

_____

_____

_____

_____

_____

_____

_____

_____

_____

_____

_____

_____

_____

_____

_____

_____

_____

_____
_____
_____
_____
_____
_____
_____
_____
_____
_____
_____
_____
_____
_____
_____
_____
_____
_____
_____

Kind Words
Matter.

What's in Your Thought Bubble Today?

DATE:

_____

_____

_____

_____

_____

_____

_____

_____

_____

_____

_____

_____

_____

_____

_____

_____

_____

_____

Smile Every Chance You Get.

What's in Your Thought Bubble Today?

DATE:

_____

_____

_____

_____

_____

_____

_____

_____

_____

_____

_____

_____

_____

_____

_____

_____

_____

_____

Value Your
Creativity & Ideas.

What's in Your Thought Bubble Today?

DATE:

Plant Something
& Watch It Grow.

What's in Your Thought Bubble Today?

DATE:

Rest Renews
Your Mind.

What's in Your Thought Bubble Today?

DATE:

Dreams Hold
Unimaginable Beauty.

What's in Your Thought Bubble Today?

DATE:

Start a Movement...
'Change the World.

What's in Your Thought Bubble Today?

DATE:

Sing a New Song.

What's in Your Thought Bubble Today?

DATE:

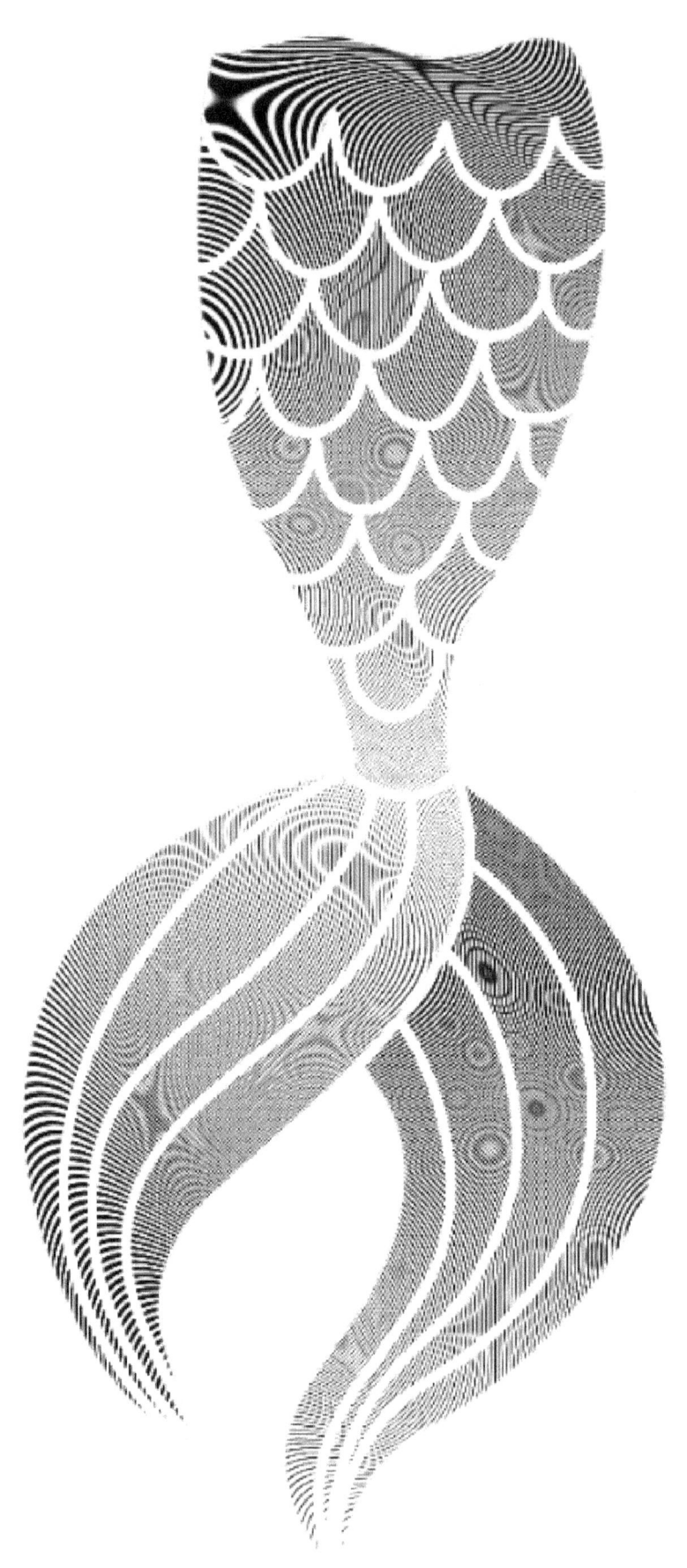

_____

_____

_____

_____

_____

_____

_____

_____

_____

_____

_____

_____

_____

_____

_____

_____

_____

_____

Genuine Friends
Are Rare & Precious.

What's in Your Thought Bubble Today?

DATE:

_____

_____

_____

_____

_____

_____

_____

_____

_____

_____

_____

_____

_____

_____

_____

_____

_____

_____

_____

Do Something Nice For Someone Today.

What's in Your Thought Bubble Today?

DATE:

You Are A Flower.
Which One?

What's in Your Thought Bubble Today?

DATE:

Challenge Yourself
Today.

What's in Your Thought Bubble Today?

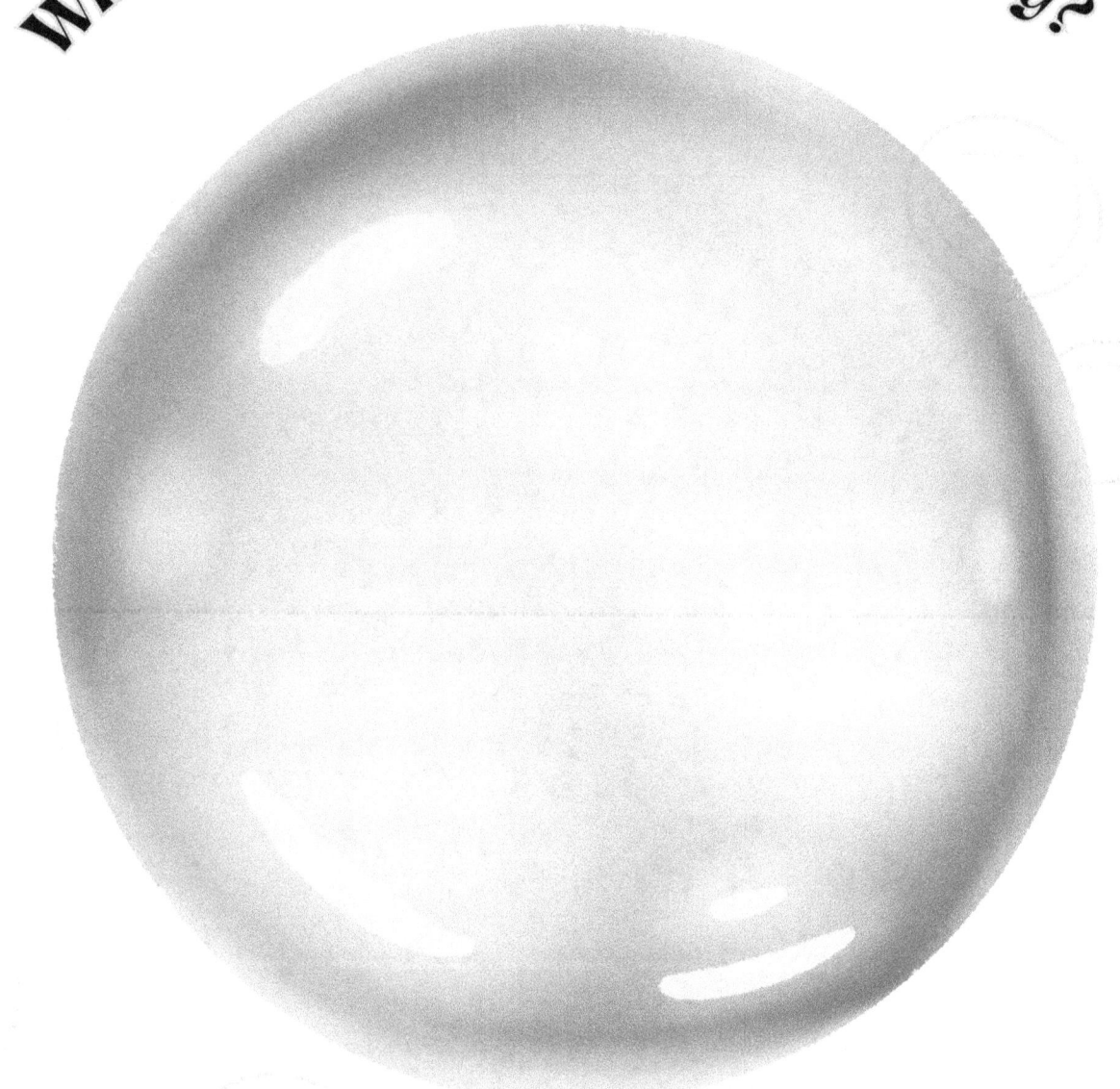

DATE:

Find Your Magic.

What's in Your Thought Bubble Today?

DATE:

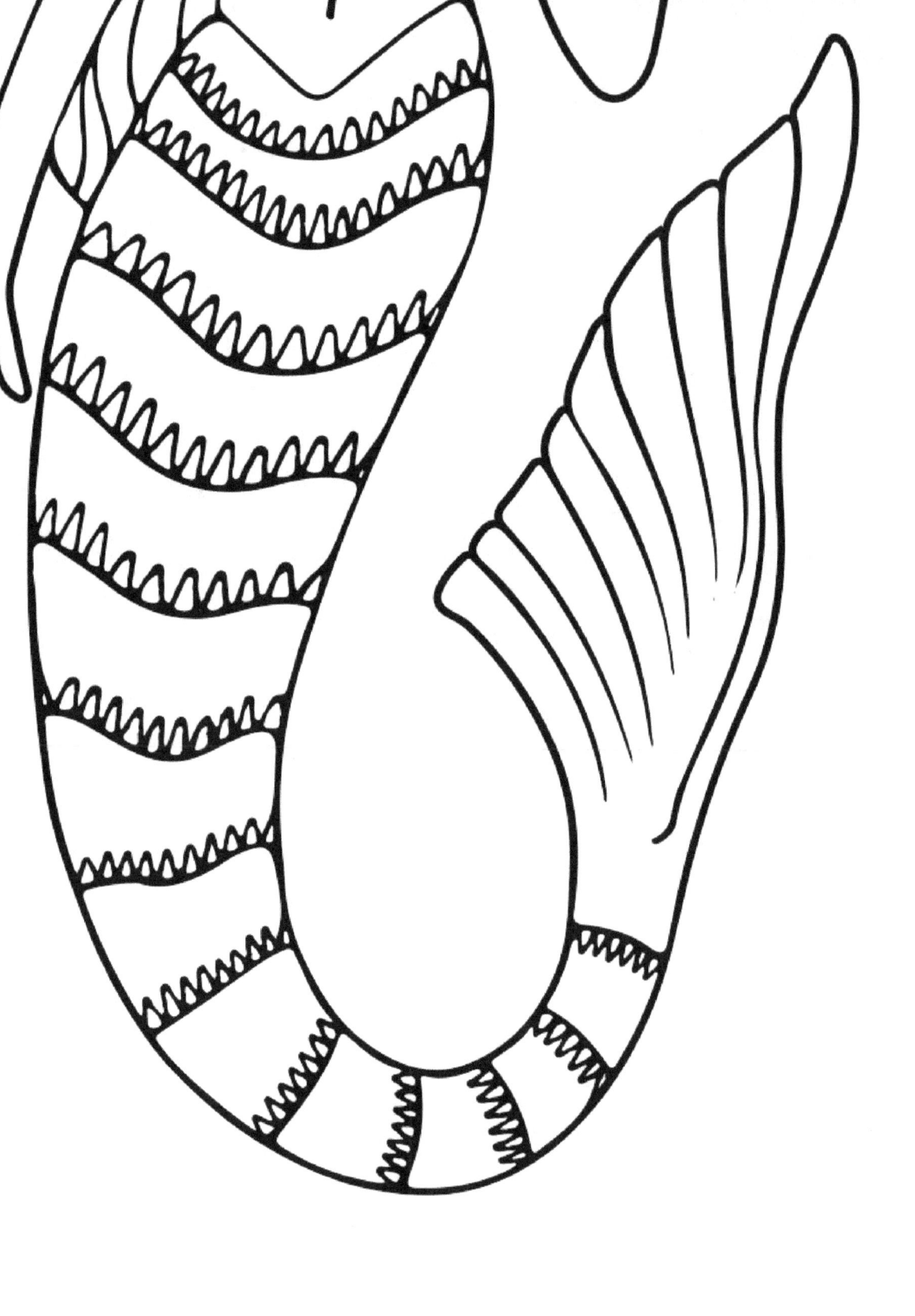

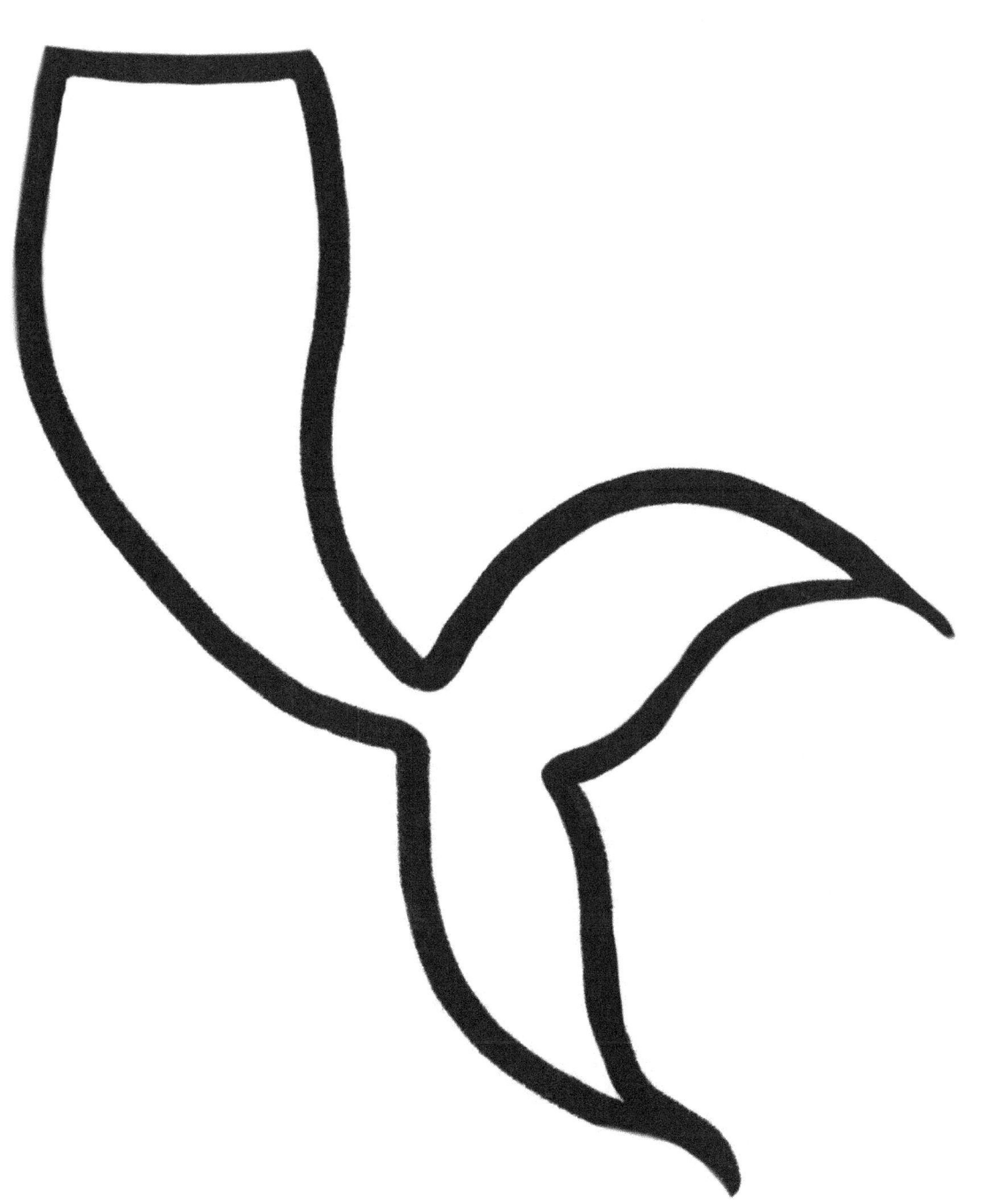

www.ingramcontent.com/pod-product-compliance
Lightning Source LLC
Chambersburg PA
CBHW081001120626
46546CB00010B/2987